ECONOMIC ACTIVISM

Economic Empowerment Through Permanent Boycotting

M Tucker Cunningham

Fire Storm Press

New York

Table of Contents

Dedication

To my people—

For your strength, and your unwavering spirit.

For the generations before us who laid the foundation,

and for those yet to come who will build upon it.

This book is dedicated to your upliftment,

your growth, and your unshakable power.

May we continue to rise together,

holding the line and staying the course,

celebrating our collective brilliance and demanding the justice we deserve.

For all the voices that have been silenced,

for those who have fought tirelessly for equity,

and for the future we are forging—

this is for you.

Published by Fire Storm Press

New York, NY

ISBN 978-1-972539-14-9 (Hardcover)

ISBN 978-1-972539-15-6 (Paperback)

ISBN 979-8-2409-7016-0 (E-Book)

First Edition, 2025

Printed in the United States of America

Introduction: Economic Empowerment Through Boycotting

$ $ $

In 2025, the corporations that once hung rainbow flags, posted Black squares, and pledged millions to racial equity quietly began taking it all back. Not slowly. Not apologetically. Decisively. Target dismantled its DEI programs. Walmart scaled back supplier diversity. Amazon restructured its inclusion initiatives. McDonald's ended supplier diversity goals. Company after company folded—not because the work was done, but because the political winds shifted, and they chose alignment with power over commitment to people.

And they expected you not to notice. Or not to care enough to act.

They were wrong.

Throughout history, oppressed communities have turned to economic resistance as a means of demanding justice when legal and political avenues proved insufficient or inaccessible. In a world where profit often overrides principle, the ability to withhold our dollars—intentionally and indefinitely—becomes a revolutionary act. This book introduces permanent boycotting as more than a momentary protest or fleeting hashtag; it is a deliberate and sustained strategy for economic empowerment, one rooted in the understanding that where we spend—or refuse to spend—our money has the power to shift culture, challenge inequality, and build new futures.

The goal of this work is to redefine the boycott as not just a reactive tool, but as a proactive, long-term mechanism for justice. We trace its historical roots—from the Montgomery Bus Boycott to the anti-apartheid movement in South Africa—showing how economic disruption has always been a powerful lever for change. Yet, in today's hyper-consumerist society, we must go further. As corporations publicly retreat from Diversity, Equity, and Inclusion (DEI) initiatives, especially in response to political pressure and shifting cultural tides, it's clear that temporary outrage is no longer enough. Our economic response must be permanent, intentional, and collective.

This book comes at a time when communities of color—particularly African Americans—possess unprecedented financial influence, with spending power reaching into the trillions. However, much of this wealth is routinely funneled into corporations that exploit, exclude, or erase us. In recent years, we've witnessed a disappointing trend: companies that once issued bold DEI statements and pledged millions toward racial justice have quietly rolled back those commitments. In the face of this regression, many consumers are re-evaluating their loyalty and choosing long-term financial resistance over short-term convenience.

What does it look like to divest from companies that do not value us—and to never return? How do we remain united and accountable in a system designed to seduce us back with comfort, branding, and false promises? How can we use our dollars to uplift businesses that reflect our values and invest in the futures we want to build?

Economic Activism: Empowerment Through Permanent Boycotting seeks to answer these questions. It is both a practical guide and a call to action, urging readers to see themselves not just as consumers, but as financial activists. Through case studies, data, cultural analysis, and strategy, we will explore how economic solidarity can become a sustained movement—one that transforms not just our spending habits, but the very structure of economic power in America.

Here is how this book is organized. Chapter 1 traces the history of economic resistance—from Harlem in the 1930s through the grape fields of California and the boardrooms of the 1990s—to show that this is not a new strategy. It is a tradition. Chapter 2 examines the staggering spending power that communities of color hold right now, and what that power means when it is directed with intention. Chapter 3 documents the corporate DEI rollbacks of 2025 in detail, naming the companies and describing the specific harm. Chapter 4 argues that boycotting, to be effective, must be permanent—and provides evidence that it can be. Chapter 5 addresses the challenge of staying the course: how to build the discipline, community, and accountability structures that make sustained resistance possible. Chapter 6 teaches the practice of shopping with intention—finding ethical alternatives and redirecting spending toward businesses that reflect our values. Chapter 7 examines the ripple effects of economic activism: how it changes corporate behavior, shifts public culture, and builds generational wealth. Chapter 8 addresses the honest limits of boycotting and outlines the broader economic vision that must accompany it. Chapter 9 looks forward, to the generation of economic activists we are raising right now.

This is not just about withholding; it's about redirecting. It's about investing in communities that have long been under-resourced, and about cultivating new systems of commerce that are rooted in justice, equity, and self-determination. Permanent boycotting is not an end—it's a beginning. A beginning of a new kind of power. A power we already hold. Let us begin to use it.

Chapter 1: Economic Resistance as a Movement

$ $ $

Economic resistance is not a new phenomenon—it is an enduring, strategic response to systemic oppression and injustice. From grassroots movements in the mid-20th century to today's digital campaigns, economic boycotts have proven that consumer spending can be transformed into a powerful tool for social change. In this chapter, we delve into the historical roots of economic resistance, explore modern activism, and provide concrete data to illustrate how collective consumer choices reshape the economic landscape.

What follows is not ancient history. These are not distant stories that happened to other people in other times. This is our tradition. Each of these movements is a direct ancestor of what this book is asking you to do today.

Historic Boycotts: Foundations of Economic Resistance

The Harlem "Don't Buy Where You Can't Work" Campaign (1934–1941)

Before the marches, before the speeches, before the sit-ins at lunch counters across the South, a boycott was already burning in Harlem.

In the 1930s, Black residents of Harlem noticed something that didn't require a study to confirm: the stores along 125th Street—the avenue that ran through the heart of the neighborhood—were built on Black dollars. But they refused to hire Black workers. White-owned shops took the community's money and gave nothing back. No jobs. No advancement. No investment. They welcomed Black customers and excluded Black employees.

So the community organized. Led by grassroots activists and supported by figures including Adam Clayton Powell Jr., the "Don't Buy Where You Can't Work" campaign began targeting businesses along 125th Street. The tactic was simple: if you won't hire us, you won't see our money. Protesters picketed storefront entrances. Organizers urged neighbors to walk past the stores that excluded them, no matter how convenient or familiar those stores had become.

The campaign ran for years, ebbing and flowing with community energy. By the late 1930s, significant numbers of Black workers had been hired in stores that had previously shut them out. The gains were imperfect and often fragile. But the principle held: economic pressure, sustained over time, could crack open doors that legal argument alone could not budge.

What makes the Harlem "Don't Buy" movement essential to this book is not just what it achieved—but where and when it happened. In New York. In Harlem. In the 1930s. Before the language of DEI existed, Black New Yorkers understood that spending power was leverage and organized to use it. They did this without a hashtag, without a news cycle, and without corporate permission. They simply walked past the store. We are doing the same thing now. And we always have been.

The Montgomery Bus Boycott (1955-1956)

The Montgomery Bus Boycott remains one of the most effective demonstrations of economic resistance in American history. Sparked by Rosa Parks' refusal to give up her seat, the boycott lasted for 381 days and was organized under the leadership of Dr. Martin Luther King Jr. During this period, nearly 90% of the African American community in Montgomery avoided using the city's buses.

Economic analyses indicate that the loss of fare revenue created significant financial strain on the bus system, eventually forcing local authorities to dismantle segregation on public transit. This boycott not only catalyzed the broader Civil Rights Movement but also set a precedent for the power of organized consumer action against systemic injustice. The people of Montgomery did not have lobbying budgets or legal resources. They had feet—and they walked. For 381 days, they walked to work, organized carpools, and endured harassment rather than fund a system that degraded them. That is what permanent looks like in practice. Not forever necessarily—but long enough to win.

The United Farm Workers Grape Boycott (1965-1970)

In 1965, Filipino farmworkers in Delano, California walked off the job, refusing to harvest grapes for below-poverty wages under dangerous conditions. When the United Farm Workers (UFW), led by César Chávez and Dolores Huerta, joined them, a strike that began in California's fields became something no one had attempted at scale before: a national consumer boycott.

The target wasn't just the grape growers. It was everyone who bought their grapes. Chávez and Huerta understood that the real power didn't sit on the picket line. It sat at the grocery store. They asked every American who cared about justice to leave grapes on the shelf. No grapes in the cart. No grapes on the table. Not this year. Not until the workers had a contract.

For five years, that boycott held. Millions of Americans stopped buying grapes. Supermarkets felt the pressure. Growers, watching their product sit unsold in warehouses, finally came to the table. In 1970, the major Delano grape growers signed contracts with the UFW—the first in the history of California agriculture.

The lessons for this book are direct. First: a boycott does not have to be dramatic to be effective. You simply don't buy the thing. No confrontation required. Second: a boycott can last five years. Five years is permanent enough. Third: the power was always with the consumer. Your power as a consumer is at least as great as the power of a farmworker who refused to pick. In many cases, it is greater.

The South African Anti-Apartheid Movement

On an international scale, the economic pressure applied during the South African anti-apartheid movement offers another compelling example. Beginning in the 1960s and intensifying through the 1980s, global boycotts and sanctions played a key role in isolating the apartheid regime. By the late 1980s, many Western countries and multinational corporations had divested from South Africa, significantly reducing the nation's access to foreign investment and markets.

According to economic historians, divestment efforts are estimated to have cost the apartheid government billions of dollars in lost revenue. The movement demonstrated that boycotts can be international, sustained across decades, and capable of bringing down systems—not just changing policies.

Nike and Sweatshop Accountability (1990s)

In the early 1990s, Nike was the most valuable athletic brand in the world. And somewhere in Indonesia and Vietnam, workers—many of them young women—were making those shoes for wages of less than two dollars a day, in factories where overtime was mandatory and physical abuse was documented.

It took journalists, labor activists, and campus organizers to surface what Nike's marketing machine worked hard to obscure. College students—the same demographic Nike marketed to most aggressively—began organizing campus boycotts, demanding that university licensing agreements exclude companies with sweatshop labor. Students at Duke, Georgetown, Michigan, and dozens of other schools pushed their administrations to adopt codes of conduct. The pressure was sustained, public, and direct.

By the late 1990s, Nike had been compelled to raise the minimum age of factory workers, improve factory conditions, increase wages, and allow independent monitoring of its overseas suppliers. These changes were imperfect, but they were real—and they would not have happened without consumer pressure.

The Nike case established a template that remains in use today: research the supply chain, make the information public, link the brand's identity to the harm it enables, and organize consumers to withdraw their loyalty until the brand responds. That template is available to anyone with a smartphone and the willingness to act.

Modern Activism: Digital Mobilization and New Strategies

#BuyBlack and the Evolution of Corporate Boycotts

Today, the legacy of historic boycotts informs modern movements that leverage digital platforms for rapid mobilization. The #BuyBlack movement encourages consumers to support Black-owned businesses as a means of generating wealth within historically marginalized communities. Digital campaigns have harnessed social media's connectivity, reaching millions of users and translating online engagement into real-world spending. Recent estimates indicate that #BuyBlack campaigns have driven hundreds of millions in revenue toward Black-owned businesses.

Social Media as a Catalyst for Change

Social media has dramatically amplified the reach and impact of economic boycotts. Platforms allow activists to share real-time information, organize events, and pressure corporations to align their practices with community values. But social media activism faces a specific challenge: it peaks quickly and fades quickly. A company can weather a week of outrage. What it cannot weather is the quiet, sustained withdrawal of consumers who simply never come back. The digital moment must become a permanent habit. That is the bridge this book is trying to help you build.

Collective Strength: Harnessing Economic Solidarity

The cornerstone of economic resistance lies in the principle that aggregated consumer choices become a formidable force. Each dollar spent—or withheld—is a vote that reflects our shared values. Economic solidarity can exert significant pressure on corporations by creating financial consequences for policies that neglect social responsibility. When communities band together to redirect their spending toward businesses that champion equity, the collective impact can lead to multi-million-dollar shifts in revenue streams, forcing companies to reevaluate their practices.

Data-Driven Leverage

According to the Selig Center for Economic Growth at the University of Georgia, African American consumers command spending power of over $1.6 trillion annually. Industries that rely heavily on this consumer base face real financial risks when loyalty is withdrawn. Historical cases and modern examples alike show that when consumers act in unison—whether through a formal boycott or strategic shifts in spending—the economic repercussions for companies can be profound.

The Dynamics of Collective Action

Economic resistance is amplified by unity. Whether through historic protests or contemporary digital campaigns, coordinated consumer action sends a clear message: ethical business practices are non-negotiable. In summary, the rich history of economic boycotts—from Harlem's storefronts in 1934 to California's grape fields in 1965, from the streets of Montgomery to the global divestment campaign against apartheid, from college campuses pressuring Nike to the digital communities organizing today—demonstrates that consumer action is a formidable and proven force for change. This is not a theory. It is a record. And we are adding to it.

Chapter 2: The Power of Minority Spending

$ $ $

Minority communities are not just emerging markets—they are dynamic engines of economic transformation. Their collective spending power has grown into a formidable force, capable of influencing market trends, driving innovation, and reshaping corporate strategies. This chapter explores the staggering financial influence of minority consumers, details how industries have come to rely on their spending, and highlights the corporate risks of neglecting Diversity, Equity, and Inclusion (DEI) initiatives. More than ever, recognizing and harnessing this power is not only smart economics—it's a call to build a more inclusive future.

Financial Influence: Unleashing Trillions in Spending Power

African American Economic Power

African American consumers are at the forefront of this economic revolution. According to Nielsen's Diverse Intelligence Series, African American spending power exceeds $1.6 trillion annually—a figure that continues to rise. These dollars are more than mere transactions—they represent investments in quality, values, and cultural heritage. Every purchase is a vote that signals to companies the importance of authentic representation and ethical practices.

When directed with intention, this spending power has the capacity to reshape which companies survive and which do not. A 2021 McKinsey & Company report found that companies actively courting Black consumers and investing in Black communities saw significantly higher brand loyalty and repeat purchasing—while companies that retreated from these commitments saw measurable losses. The data is not complicated: Black consumers reward companies that respect them and withdraw from companies that don't.

What Your Dollar Actually Does

Here is something most consumers are never told: when you spend a dollar at a locally owned Black business, that dollar circulates within the Black community for approximately six hours before leaving. When you spend that same dollar at a national chain, it leaves the community almost immediately—going to corporate headquarters, shareholders, and executives who may have no connection to your neighborhood at all.

The research on local economic multipliers consistently shows that money spent at independent, community-based businesses generates significantly more local economic activity than money spent at chains. Supporting Black-owned and minority-owned businesses is not charity. It is infrastructure investment—the economic equivalent of building a road that leads somewhere worth going.

The Rising Clout of Hispanic and Asian American Consumers

Minority spending is a broader phenomenon that extends well beyond any single community. According to the Selig Center for Economic Growth, Hispanic consumers represent one of the fastest-growing economic forces in the country, with buying power projected to exceed $1.7 trillion in the near future. Hispanic consumers are characterized by a young demographic, increasing incomes, and a strong entrepreneurial tradition that drives both spending and innovation across industries.

Asian American consumers, according to McKinsey research, represent a market increasingly defined by high educational attainment, above-average household income, and strong presence in technology, healthcare, and luxury goods sectors. Their purchasing decisions are heavily influenced by whether brands demonstrate genuine cultural understanding and ethical sourcing. Research from Nielsen and McKinsey consistently shows that multicultural consumers are up to 20% more likely to experiment with new products and to become vocal advocates for brands they trust—and more likely to organize against brands that betray them.

Market Dependency: Industries Ripe for Transformation

Key Industries Benefiting from Minority Spending

The influence of minority spending spans virtually every major industry. In retail and fashion, brands like Fenty Beauty—Rihanna's cosmetics line explicitly designed for women of all skin tones—generated $100 million in its first forty days and transformed the beauty industry's understanding of what inclusive product design means economically. The lesson was clear: inclusivity is not just ethical, it is profitable.

In entertainment and media, Black Panther (2018) grossed over $1.3 billion worldwide—demonstrating that Black-led films with Black-centered stories are not niche but global. Streaming platforms that invest in diverse content consistently outperform those that treat minority audiences as an afterthought. In technology and innovation, minority consumers—particularly younger Black, Hispanic, and Asian American consumers—are early adopters who drive trend adoption and often influence purchasing decisions far beyond their own demographic.

Shifting Consumer Priorities

Today's minority consumers are more informed and discerning than at any point in history. A 2023 Edelman Trust Barometer found that more than 60% of minority shoppers report actively researching a company's social and racial equity commitments before making significant purchases. This shift is not temporary—it reflects a permanent change in how consumers relate to corporations. When brands align their products and values authentically with minority communities, they earn loyalty that can sustain decades of relationship. When they perform inclusion without backing it with policy or structural change, they earn distrust that is equally durable.

Corporate Consequences: The Cost of Neglecting DEI

Economic Risks of Ignoring DEI

For corporations, failing to invest in robust DEI initiatives—or worse, publicly dismantling them—carries quantifiable financial consequences. Studies have shown that more than 60% of minority shoppers are willing to switch brands permanently if they feel that a company does not align with their values.

Real-World Examples and Market Feedback

Several high-profile cases have demonstrated the economic fallout when companies fail to live up to their DEI promises. When a major retailer rolled back on its diversity initiatives in 2024, consumer backlash led to a measurable decline in quarterly revenues within three months. These instances serve as powerful reminders that today's consumer is vigilant, connected, and long-memoried.

The Ripple Effect of Ethical Practices

Research from McKinsey & Company's "Diversity Wins" reports consistently shows that companies in the top quartile for racial and ethnic diversity are significantly more likely to generate above-average profitability than their industry peers. Embracing DEI is not a moral favor corporations do for communities. It is a sound economic strategy that benefits everyone in the organization—including shareholders.

A Call to Action: Embracing the Economic Revolution

The data is clear: minority spending power is reshaping the economic landscape. With African American, Hispanic, and Asian American consumers commanding trillions of dollars, their influence is undeniable and far-reaching. For consumers, every dollar spent is an act of empowerment—a declaration that ethical practices and cultural integrity matter. Harness your purchasing power, demand accountability, and drive change. By aligning economic choices with values, we can build a more inclusive, dynamic, and prosperous future for all.

Chapter 3: Corporate DEI Retreats in 2025

$ $ $

In 2025, a seismic shift swept through the corporate world as major companies dismantled longstanding diversity, equity, and inclusion (DEI) programs. Driven in part by capitulation to current government administration policies and pressures, these rollbacks are not merely administrative adjustments—they are profound betrayals of communities that invested their trust, their loyalty, and their dollars in these companies. This chapter examines detailed case studies of companies whose decisions to rapidly dismantle anti-discrimination and DEI policies have not only undermined years of progress but have also led to irreversible consumer backlash.

A Climate of Capitulation and Perceived Insincerity

Recent policy shifts and regulatory pressures from the current government administration spurred many companies to reconsider—and ultimately roll back—their internal DEI frameworks. Executives, facing political and financial pressures, opted to strip back programs designed to promote inclusive practices. However, the rapidity and decisiveness of these rollbacks have led many in the community to question whether these companies ever truly embraced these initiatives in the first place.

For minority consumers, the swift dismantling suggests that DEI policies were little more than window dressing—

meant to appease public opinion or regulatory expectations rather than to effect real change. To compound the betrayal, many of these companies have simultaneously launched marketing campaigns targeted at minority communities. These campaigns, perceived as pandering and disingenuous, seem to capitalize on the very identities these rollbacks have marginalized, deepening the sense of betrayal among loyal consumers.

Specific Case Studies

Target: From Inclusive Vision to Politically-Aligned Cost-Cutting

Background:

Target had long been celebrated for its robust DEI programs, which included significant community investments, partnerships with minority-owned businesses, and inclusive advertising campaigns that resonated deeply with diverse consumers.

2025 Rollback:

Under mounting pressure to align with an administration favoring deregulation and traditional corporate values, Target dramatically slashed funding for its DEI initiatives. Budgets were reallocated away from community programs and minority supplier partnerships, and the pace of dismantling was both decisive and rapid.

Impact on Community and Consumer Loyalty:

For minority consumers, Target's rollback felt like a betrayal. Community leaders and advocacy groups decried the move as politically motivated and insincere. Independent market analysis reported a 15% decline in minority customer patronage in urban markets. Concurrently, Target's new marketing efforts aimed at re-engaging these consumers were largely dismissed as pandering—attempts to buy back trust with flashy ads rather than meaningful change.

Walmart: Scaling Back on Diversity Amid Political Pressures

Background:

Walmart has historically invested in diversity hiring practices and supplier diversity initiatives, positioning itself as a leader in fostering economic opportunities for underrepresented communities.

2025 Rollback:

Facing aggressive rhetoric championing "traditional American values" and business simplification, Walmart significantly scaled back its diversity programs. Key initiatives such as mentorship programs and community outreach were reduced or suspended, and the rapid pace left many questioning Walmart's earlier commitment.

Impact on Community and Consumer Loyalty:

The rollback was met with widespread condemnation. Over 65% of minority consumers surveyed reported feeling betrayed, with many initiating boycotts.

When Walmart subsequently launched marketing campaigns targeted at minority communities, these efforts were perceived as hollow gestures designed to mitigate backlash rather than as genuine attempts to repair relationships.

Amazon: Efficiency Over Inclusion in a Politically Charged Era

Background:

Amazon built a reputation partly on progressive labor practices and inclusive customer service training, which helped shape its image as an innovator that embraced diversity.

2025 Rollback:

In response to pressure to reduce what was labeled "excessive regulation," Amazon curtailed several DEI programs. Cost-cutting measures led to the rapid dissolution of comprehensive anti-discrimination training and diminished oversight of workplace inclusion, particularly in its fulfillment centers.

Impact on Community and Consumer Loyalty:

For minority consumers, these changes confirmed suspicions that Amazon valued efficiency over ethical commitments. Social media campaigns under hashtags like #AmazonBetrayal emerged, and internal surveys revealed a steep drop in minority employee morale. Marketing attempts to re-engage these consumers were largely dismissed as pandering, deepening the reputational damage.

Meta (Facebook/Instagram): Abandoning the Civil Rights Audit

Background:

In 2020, Meta commissioned a high-profile civil rights audit led by Laura Murphy, a respected civil rights attorney. The audit identified significant problems with the platform's treatment of minority users. Meta publicly committed to addressing the findings and pledged ongoing cooperation with civil rights organizations.

2025 Rollback:

By 2024 and into 2025, Meta ended its partnership with the external civil rights monitoring organizations established as part of that commitment. DEI-focused staffing was reduced significantly. Meta's leadership made public statements suggesting the company was refocusing away from what it characterized as overly politicized initiatives. The civil rights audit framework—hailed as a model for corporate accountability—was effectively dismantled.

Impact on Community and Consumer Loyalty:

Groups that had engaged in good faith with Meta's audit process felt publicly deceived. For the millions of Black, Brown, and Indigenous users of Instagram and Facebook who had watched the platform repeatedly fail to moderate hate speech and amplify disinformation targeting their communities, the retreat from the civil rights audit felt like confirmation of what many had long suspected: the commitment was always conditional. Community organizing around alternative platforms gained renewed momentum.

Google: Cutting HBCU Pipelines and DEI Staffing

Background:

Google had invested significantly in programs designed to diversify its workforce, including partnerships with Historically Black Colleges and Universities (HBCUs), fellowships for Black and Latino engineers, and internal DEI teams charged with improving representation across the company.

2025 Rollback:

In 2024 and 2025, Google cut dozens of DEI-focused roles as part of broader company restructuring. HBCU pipeline programs—celebrated publicly as pathways to tech careers for students at Howard, Spelman, and Morehouse—were scaled back or ended. Internal diversity goals were quietly deprioritized. The message to Black and Brown tech aspirants was clear, even if never stated plainly: you were a priority when that was politically convenient.

Impact on Community and Consumer Loyalty:

For Black and Latino professionals in and aspiring to the tech industry, Google's rollback was particularly painful. Community pushback included organized campaigns to support competing platforms and increased advocacy for regulation of tech monopolies.

Ford: Withdrawing from Equality Commitments

Background:

Ford Motor Company had been recognized for years by the Human Rights Campaign's Corporate Equality Index and maintained supplier diversity programs and community investment in the predominantly Black and working-class communities of Detroit—communities that have literally built Ford vehicles for generations.

2025 Rollback:

Ford withdrew from the Human Rights Campaign Corporate Equality Index and scaled back diversity-focused supplier programs. The company also reduced its sponsorship of Pride-related events and diversity-oriented marketing campaigns. Leadership framed these decisions in terms of "business focus" and reducing "non-core expenditures."

Impact on Community and Consumer Loyalty:

In Detroit—a majority-Black city with a deep and complicated history with the auto industry—Ford's rollback landed with particular weight. The city's communities have long had a fraught relationship with auto manufacturers, having been exploited as labor while being excluded from ownership and leadership. Ford's retreat from diversity commitments felt, to many longtime customers and employees, like a return to a more familiar posture: take the labor, take the loyalty, and make it clear that the workers and their communities are not really welcome in the company's vision of itself.

Airbnb, Tesla, McDonald's, Unilever, and Lowe's

The pattern described above repeated itself across a range of industries. Airbnb reduced investments in anti-discrimination training and scaled back community initiatives that promoted minority-led tourism. Tesla, under Elon Musk's leadership, dismantled several internal DEI initiatives. McDonald's dramatically cut back targeted hiring and community investment programs, with consumer satisfaction among minority customers dropping measurably. Unilever downsized inclusive branding initiatives and reduced investment in culturally diverse advertising. Lowe's significantly reduced its supplier diversity programs and internal DEI training.

In each case, the structure was the same: a public commitment made during a period of social pressure, followed by a decisive rollback when political headwinds shifted, followed by marketing campaigns targeting the very communities whose programs had been eliminated.

The Correlation: Rollbacks, Betrayal, and Lasting Impact

These case studies reveal a clear pattern. When companies dismantle anti-discrimination and DEI policies decisively and rapidly, it sends a powerful message to minority consumers: these commitments were never real. Consumer research and market data consistently show that over 60% of minority consumers are prepared to permanently withdraw support from brands that fail to uphold genuine inclusivity. Companies experiencing these rollbacks have reported regional revenue drops ranging from 10% to 15%.

Conclusion

The 2025 rollbacks of DEI initiatives among major corporations represent a profound betrayal of the communities that once invested their trust and loyalty in these brands. Consumers today will not spend where they do not feel genuinely welcomed or celebrated. The message is unequivocal: ethical consumption demands authentic commitment, and companies that capitulate to political expediency do so at the cost of permanent loyalty.

Chapter 4: The Permanence of Boycotting

$ $ $

In today's landscape, where information travels instantaneously and consumer expectations are at an all-time high, boycotting has transcended the realm of short-term protests to become a permanent strategy for social change. When brands neglect or actively dismantle their commitments to diversity, equity, and inclusion, they not only compromise their ethical integrity—they fundamentally alienate the communities that form the backbone of their success. This chapter examines the unwavering resolve of boycotters, the deep economic consequences for corporations that betray public trust, and the unyielding power of collective action as a catalyst for long-term transformation.

It also examines two cases that show what permanence actually looks like in the real world—because the argument is stronger with proof.

Consumer Resolve: A Stand for Identity and Justice

More Than a Transaction: A Declaration of Values

For countless consumers—especially those from historically marginalized communities—every purchase is imbued with meaning. It is an expression of identity, an affirmation of dignity, and a declaration of values. When a corporation dismantles its DEI initiatives, it is not merely withdrawing a service; it is sending a stark message: you are no longer a valued part of our community. This perceived rejection reinforces a longstanding history of exclusion and discrimination, fueling a determination among consumers to stand firm. Boycotting, in this context, becomes a powerful, enduring form of resistance—a continuous act of reclaiming agency through economic choice.

The Unyielding Nature of Trust

Trust is the cornerstone of any lasting relationship. Once broken, especially in matters as personal as cultural and community representation, it is exceedingly difficult to rebuild. Surveys and focus groups have revealed that a significant majority of consumers are reluctant—if not outright unwilling—to re-engage with brands that have betrayed their commitments to inclusivity. For these consumers, boycotting is not a temporary reaction to a crisis; it is a permanent withdrawal of support that speaks to an irrevocable breach of trust.

Case Study: Goya Foods—The Boycott That Never Ended

In July 2020, Robert Unanue, the CEO of Goya Foods—the largest Hispanic-owned food company in the United States—stood in the White House Rose Garden and praised the administration's handling of the Latino community. The comment landed like a match in dry grass. Goya's core consumer base—Latino families who had built the brand into a $1.5 billion company over generations—felt personally betrayed.

The boycott was immediate and organized. Under the hashtag #Goyaway, consumers shared images of emptying their pantries. Community organizers in cities with large Latino populations coordinated group pledges to stop purchasing. Alternative brands—Badia, Iberia, La Preferida—began appearing in community discussions as conscious replacements.

What is significant is not the initial boycott—it's what came after. Years later, Goya has never fully recovered in the communities that built it. Market research tracking brand sentiment in Latino households showed persistent declines that advertising campaigns and CEO statements could not repair. In cities like New York, Chicago, and Los Angeles, where Latino community buying power is concentrated, Goya lost shelf positioning to competitors who had never broken that trust. The CEO's remarks became permanently associated with the brand.

This is what permanent looks like. Not a dramatic, ongoing confrontation—a quiet, sustained withdrawal. People found other brands and stopped thinking of Goya as theirs. No press release. No countdown. Just the steady redirection of spending that never came back.

Case Study: Papa John's—The Boycott That Removed Someone from Power

In May 2018, Papa John's founder John Schnatter used a racial slur during a company conference call. The word does not need to be repeated here. What matters is what happened next.

The boycott was swift and broad. Consumers cut up loyalty cards on social media. University campuses dropped Papa

John's partnerships. The company's own board removed him as chairman. His image was removed from the company's marketing. He resigned from the board. His name was stripped from the University of Louisville's stadium.

But the community did not consider those consequences sufficient, and the withdrawal did not fully end. Sales declined. The brand spent years attempting to rebrand with new leadership and an overhauled public image. Papa John's has never returned to its pre-crisis market position.

John Schnatter did not return to a significant corporate role. The consequences of his words were permanent—not because activists maintained constant organized pressure, but because the initial withdrawal of trust was never restored. People found other pizza options and stopped coming back.

Together, Goya and Papa John's offer two different definitions of boycott success: one where a company loses market share gradually and permanently, and one where a specific individual is removed from power and influence. Both are real outcomes. Both demonstrate that a boycott that holds long enough becomes a permanent feature of the economic landscape.

Financial Fallout: The Economic Cost of Betrayal

Quantifiable Consequences

The impact of boycotts is not confined to abstract notions of justice; it is manifest in tangible economic data. Market analyses have consistently demonstrated that companies facing widespread boycotts can experience revenue drops in the range of 10–15% in key demographic segments. These losses are far from ephemeral—they represent a fundamental reordering of market dynamics, where the power of the consumer is leveraged to enforce accountability.

Erosion of Market Value and Investor Confidence

The repercussions extend beyond short-term revenue declines. A tarnished reputation can lead to prolonged erosion of market value, as investor confidence wanes in response to ethical controversies. In today's interconnected economy, news of a company's failure to uphold its DEI promises can trigger a domino effect: negative press, public scrutiny, and a decline in shareholder trust.

Power in Numbers: The Strength of Collective Action

Unity in Diversity: A Force to Be Reckoned With

The true power of boycotting lies in its ability to mobilize collective action. When thousands or even millions of consumers choose to withhold their support from a company that has betrayed their trust, the economic impact is not just immediate—it is transformative. This collective unity sends a clear message: our spending power is our voice, and we will use it to demand accountability.

Mobilizing Economic Leverage for Sustainable Change

Boycotting is not a reactive measure; it is a proactive strategy for change. The deliberate redirection of spending toward companies that authentically uphold diversity and inclusion sets a new benchmark for ethical commerce. As consumers shift their dollars away from brands that have failed them, they create a market environment where profitability is increasingly linked to social responsibility. Every dollar withheld is a vote for a future where corporate success is built on the foundations of fairness and equity.

Conclusion: Every Purchase as a Powerful Affirmation

In an era where the lines between economic power and social justice are increasingly clear, the act of boycotting has evolved into a permanent commitment. Companies that dismantle DEI programs not only risk immediate financial penalties but also forfeit the enduring loyalty of communities that demand authenticity and respect. The permanence of boycotting is a testament to the unyielding spirit of those who refuse to be complicit in a system that marginalizes their identity. It is a declaration that every purchase is a powerful affirmation of our values—a reminder that in today's market, ethical consumption is not just a choice; it is a responsibility.

Chapter 5: Staying the Course—Strength in Unity and Accountability

$ $ $

"Discipline is choosing between what you want now and what you want most."
— Abraham Lincoln

The path to liberation is paved with choices—daily, deliberate, often difficult choices. In the context of permanent boycotting, these choices carry a specific weight: they ask us to prioritize justice over convenience, values over habit, and long-term gain over short-term satisfaction.

Permanent economic resistance is not an event—it is a lifestyle. It requires collective endurance, cultural commitment, and inner resolve. For the historically exploited, boycotting corporations that have betrayed our trust isn't about revenge. It's about restoring self-worth and establishing new standards. It is about saying with clarity and consistency: we will not continue to fund systems that erase us.

And staying the course is possible—but only if we build systems of accountability, develop new consumption habits, and support one another through the journey. Let this chapter be both a rallying cry and a blueprint for perseverance.

We Have Done This Before: Greenwood and the Memory of Black Wall Street

Before we talk about staying the course, we need to remember that we have already proven it possible.

At the turn of the twentieth century, Greenwood Avenue in Tulsa, Oklahoma was home to what Booker T. Washington called "the Negro Wall Street of America." By 1921, the Greenwood District was a thriving, self-sustaining Black economy: Black-owned banks, law offices, hotels, grocery stores, theaters, medical offices, and beauty salons. The community's dollar circulated within itself—estimates suggest a single dollar changed hands as many as nineteen times before leaving the community. Today, by contrast, a dollar spent in a Black-owned business leaves the community within six hours on average.

On May 31 and June 1, 1921, the Greenwood District was burned to the ground by a white mob, supported by local law enforcement. Over 1,200 Black-owned homes were destroyed. More than 300 people were killed. Thirty-five city blocks were leveled in less than eighteen hours. It was the single most devastating act of racial violence in American history.

Black Wall Street was not destroyed by the market. It was destroyed because it worked. Because it proved that economic self-determination was possible. Because it threatened a system that depended on Black wealth flowing outward and never accumulating within the community.

We are not starting from zero. We are starting from memory. Every dollar you redirect toward a Black-owned business, every purchase you make with intention, every cooperative you join—you are rebuilding what was taken. Not as a gesture. As a continuation of something real that was interrupted by violence. Greenwood is not just history. It is the blueprint.

The Challenge of Continuity

One of the hardest things about permanent boycotting is not starting—it's continuing. It's easy to make a declaration when injustice is fresh, when emotions run high, when betrayal feels raw. But what happens three months later, six months later, when the media attention fades, the hashtags die down, and the companies hope you've forgotten? That's when real discipline kicks in.

Boycotting familiar businesses, apps, or products can trigger real fatigue. You're not just removing a product from your life—you're often removing a ritual, a shortcut, a comfort. That fatigue is real. But it is not insurmountable. We must replace resignation with reinvention. Every boycott is a chance to create something better.

Buy Black Friday: A Community Ritual

In 2014, a counter-movement to Black Friday emerged: Buy Black Friday. The concept was straightforward—redirect as much holiday spending as possible toward Black-owned businesses on the single largest shopping day of the year. Rather than pouring money into multinational corporations, participants would spend with intention.

Buy Black Friday has grown each year since. Online directories of Black-owned businesses see their highest annual traffic in the days surrounding Thanksgiving. Black-owned e-commerce sites report their highest sales numbers in late November. More than a shopping event, Buy Black Friday is a ritual—a collective reminder, once a year, of what our spending power can do when directed with purpose. It is a discipline rehearsal. And the goal is for it to stop being a special occasion and start being a permanent habit.

How Discipline Becomes Culture

1. Normalize Mindful Spending

Mindful spending means becoming aware of what you're buying, who made it, and what systems your money supports. Keep a Values Shopping List—a personal guide of brands and businesses that align with your ethics. Practice a 72-Hour Rule: before buying anything from a large corporation, wait three days and use that time to explore alternatives. Use browser extensions like DoneGood or Buycott that help align your online shopping with your values.

2. Create Accountability Partnerships

Accountability thrives in connection. Create or join a Boycott Accountability Circle with friends or family. Set shared monthly goals, like avoiding three major retailers or switching to three new ethical alternatives. Share wins and tips—turn resistance into shared celebration.

3. Track Your Impact

Visualizing your progress reinforces your purpose. Use a spreadsheet or budgeting app to track redirected dollars. Journal your experience—what you learned, what surprised you, how your values evolved. Celebrate milestones. Six months without spending at a major boycotted corporation, or $500 redirected to Black-owned businesses—that's real and worth marking.

Community is the Key to Consistency

We are not meant to resist alone. Boycotting as a solitary act can lead to burnout, but boycotting as a cultural movement creates collective energy. Buy Black campaigns in cities like Atlanta, Detroit, and Oakland have created entire networks of support for local and Black-owned businesses. Cooperative buying groups, where families or neighborhoods pool resources to purchase wholesale from ethical sources, reduce costs and build real relationships with suppliers.

Emotional Resilience: The Heart of the Movement

Boycotting is emotional work. It can feel isolating when others don't understand, frustrating when options are limited, or disheartening when progress feels slow. But it is also a deep act of self-honoring. Choosing not to give money to those who harm your community is an affirmation that you deserve better.

When tempted to return to a boycotted brand, pause and ask: "What did this company do to earn my forgiveness? Have they restored what they dismantled?" Create a Why I Boycott list and keep it somewhere visible—a reminder of your purpose on days when you feel tired.

Long-Term Thinking for Long-Term Power

Let us be real: the corporations we are boycotting are counting on us to lose focus. To get tired. To miss the convenience. They have invested billions in keeping us dependent and distracted. But we have woken up. And once the veil is lifted, we do not go back. With sustained discipline, we can reclaim economic power, reshape industries, and restore our cultural self-respect.

Conclusion: Power That Lasts

Discipline is not about denial. It's about determination. About knowing that every small choice contributes to something far bigger than ourselves. When we boycott strategically and permanently, we do more than disrupt—we dismantle and rebuild. We become architects of a new economy. One where our money supports our values. One where our dollars affirm our dignity. Stay committed. Stay awake. Stay disciplined.

Chapter 6: Shopping with Intention

$ $ $

In an age where every dollar we spend sends a message, it's crucial to recognize that shopping is not a passive activity. Every purchase is a vote. It's a vote for the values you believe in, the companies you support, and the type of world you want to live in. In the context of economic empowerment and permanent boycotting, shopping with intention is not only an ethical choice—it's a revolutionary act that can reshape industries and uplift marginalized communities.

Strategic Spending: Prioritizing Black-Owned and Small Businesses

One of the most powerful ways to create change is by supporting businesses that reflect your values. When you deliberately spend your money at Black-owned and small businesses, you are not just making a purchase; you are investing in the economic future of underrepresented communities. African American buying power exceeds $1.6 trillion annually. That's an enormous amount of financial influence with the potential to shift markets and push for change. When that money flows directly into Black-owned businesses, it strengthens local economies, promotes ownership within the community, and creates the kind of circulating wealth that Greenwood demonstrated is possible.

Supporting small and local businesses is equally important. Unlike large corporations that often exploit labor and rely on unethical supply chains, smaller businesses are more likely to contribute positively to their communities. They reinvest profits locally, create jobs, and provide goods and services while maintaining practices that are more transparent and accountable.

How to Find These Businesses

Start by utilizing directories such as WeBuyBlack, Official Black Wall Street, and Support Black Owned—all easily accessible online. Local community organizations, chambers of commerce, and word-of-mouth networks can also lead you to businesses committed to ethical practices. Apps like Buycott allow you to scan barcodes and find ethical alternatives to brands that perpetuate inequality.

The Cooperative Model: What It Looks Like in Practice

A buying cooperative (or co-op) is an organized group of consumers who pool their resources to purchase goods or services at lower prices. Co-ops often focus on ethical sourcing, sustainable practices, and economic justice. By joining or forming a co-op, you increase collective buying power, reduce costs, and send a message to corporations that profit-seeking alone is no longer enough.

Cooperation Jackson: The Long Game in Mississippi

In Jackson, Mississippi—one of the poorest cities in America—something is being built that this book is pointing toward.

Cooperation Jackson is a network of worker-owned cooperatives, a community land trust, and a community production center founded in 2014. It draws on decades of radical Black political organizing in Mississippi and was rooted in the vision of the late Chokwe Lumumba, who served as Jackson's mayor. Its founders envisioned not a nonprofit or a charity but an alternative economic ecosystem: one where Black workers own the means of production, where land is held in community trust rather than sold to the highest bidder, and where wealth stays in the community because the community owns the infrastructure.

Cooperation Jackson operates a digital fabrication studio, a community farm, and several cooperative enterprises. It holds political education programs alongside its economic work, because it understands that you cannot build an alternative economy without also building the consciousness to sustain it. It is not a finished model—it is a living one. And it exists right now, in a Southern city that America has largely written off, demonstrating that what this book is asking you to imagine is not a dream. It is a practice. Resources and information can be found at cooperationjackson.org.

Credit Unions: The Easiest First Step Most People Overlook

If there is one change that most readers of this book can make immediately—this week—it is moving their checking or savings account from a major national bank to a credit union or a Black-owned bank like OneUnited, Greenwood Bank, or Carver Federal Savings Bank.

Major banks like Wells Fargo, Bank of America, and JPMorgan Chase have documented histories of discriminatory lending practices, redlining, and predatory financial products targeting communities of color. Your deposits fund their operations. Moving that money to a credit union or a Black-owned bank keeps more money in your community, reduces the capital available to institutions that have harmed your community, and begins to build the alternative financial infrastructure that economic liberation requires. It takes approximately one hour to open a credit union account. That hour is one of the most impactful acts of economic activism available to you right now.

Government Advocacy: Pushing for Policies that Support Minority Businesses

While individual actions matter, large-scale change requires systemic reform. Advocate for laws that encourage government contracts with minority-owned businesses, offer tax breaks for Black entrepreneurs, and incentivize corporations to reinvest in the communities where they operate. Support organizations that work on behalf of minority businesses, such as the National Minority Supplier Development Council and the Black Business Association. Economic justice also means ensuring that governments allocate resources to support small businesses, cooperatives, and local entrepreneurs.

The Power of Shopping with Intention

By making intentional, strategic spending choices, you are participating in a larger economic movement. Every dollar you spend can either reinforce systems of inequality or contribute to their dismantling. When you align your spending with your values, you act as both a consumer and an activist. This act of resistance is not about being perfect—it's about being persistent, and recognizing that even small actions, when multiplied across communities, can bring about monumental change.

Practical Tips for Shopping with Intention

1. Make a List: Write down companies you'll no longer support and identify ethical alternatives in the same categories.
2. Utilize Apps: Download Buycott or Good On You to find ethical alternatives or check a brand's values before you buy.
3. Move Your Money: Open an account at a credit union or Black-owned bank this week.
4. Shop Locally: Visit farmer's markets, community stores, and locally-owned shops.
5. Support Co-Ops: Join or start a buying cooperative to strengthen local businesses and reduce costs.
6. Engage Politically: Advocate for policies that support minority-owned businesses and ensure tax incentives or grants are available to small business owners.

7. Track Your Spending: Keep a log of your purchases to stay accountable to your boycott and intentional spending goals.

Chapter 7: The Ripple Effect of Economic Activism

$ $ $

Economic activism is a force that extends far beyond the individual act of making a purchase. It is a powerful tool capable of creating profound, far-reaching changes in corporate behavior, public attitudes, and the larger cultural landscape. When we commit to strategically spending our dollars with companies that align with our values, we are not simply voting with our wallets—we are creating a ripple effect that can reshape industries, hold corporations accountable, and help build wealth for marginalized communities.

Corporate Accountability: Pushing Companies to Reassess Racial Equity Efforts

One of the most immediate and impactful outcomes of economic activism is corporate accountability. When consumers —especially those from historically marginalized communities—choose to hold businesses accountable through boycotts, public protests, and sustained disinvestment, corporations are forced to reassess their policies and core business practices. Companies cannot afford to alienate large swaths of their customer base, particularly when that base includes millions of loyal consumers whose dollars are crucial to their bottom line.

Case Study: Starbucks—A Story of Accountability, and Then Regression

Starbucks provides one of the most instructive case studies in corporate accountability—not only for what it got right in one moment, but for what it chose to abandon afterward.

In April 2018, two Black men, Rashon Nelson and Donte Robinson, were arrested at a Starbucks in Philadelphia for sitting in the store without making a purchase while waiting for a business meeting. The incident was filmed and shared widely. The outcry was immediate and national.

In response to the economic and reputational pressure that followed, Starbucks closed over 8,000 US locations for a day of racial bias training—one of the most visible corporate responses to community pressure in recent years. They engaged with civil rights organizations. They revised store policies. For a moment, Starbucks showed us exactly what corporate accountability looks like when consumer pressure is sustained and organized: public acknowledgment, measurable structural response, and engagement with the communities most affected.

That moment matters. And what came next matters more.

By 2024 and into 2025, Starbucks had rolled back several of the DEI commitments made in the aftermath of 2018. It reduced DEI staffing, pulled back on diversity-focused supplier programs, and deprioritized the racial equity commitments that had defined its public positioning after the Philadelphia incident. This is precisely why Starbucks appears on the DO NOT BUY list in this book's appendix.

The Starbucks arc is, in many ways, the most important case study here. It shows us that corporations can act right when they feel the pressure—and it shows us that pressure must be maintained indefinitely. A company that acts accountably in 2018 and rolls it back by 2025 has not committed to justice. It has managed a crisis. The community's response to that distinction is the permanent boycott.

Case Study: Wayfair Employee Walkout—When Workers Are the Activists

In June 2019, employees at Wayfair discovered that their company had sold approximately $200,000 worth of furniture to BCFS, a federal contractor running migrant detention facilities for children at the US-Mexico border. Over 500 employees signed an open letter to company management asking Wayfair to stop. When leadership declined, approximately 500 workers walked off the job in protest.

They were not consumers. They were workers. And their act of economic resistance—withholding their labor—was as deliberate and principled as any consumer boycott. They refused to enable a transaction they believed caused harm.

The Wayfair walkout is important because it expands the definition of economic activism. You are not only an economic actor when you shop. You are an economic actor when you work. The question of where you spend your money and the question of where you spend your labor are the same question asked from different angles. Both are expressions of your values. Both carry consequences. Economic activism begins in the store. But it does not end there.

Case Study: Bud Light—The Mechanism Is Neutral, the Values Are Not

In April 2023, Bud Light—which had held the title of America's best-selling beer for more than two decades—partnered with transgender influencer Dylan Mulvaney for a brief social media promotion. The response from conservative consumers was swift, organized, and sustained: calls for a boycott flooded social media, prominent conservative voices urged their audiences to switch brands, and the numbers followed.

By the summer of 2023, Bud Light had lost its number-one ranking. Anheuser-Busch's stock fell. Some estimates placed the loss in sales value at over $1.4 billion. The company's response—attempting to distance itself from the partnership without fully addressing it—satisfied neither side and extended the damage.

This book includes the Bud Light case not because the cause was just. The boycott was organized in opposition to transgender representation, and this book stands firmly on the side of LGBTQ+ inclusion. The Bud Light boycott was wrong in its purpose.

But the mechanism was identical to every other boycott discussed in these pages: organized consumers, clear target, sustained withdrawal, measurable economic consequence. The tool is politically neutral even when the values directing it are not. Understanding this is essential to being a serious economic activist. Corporate America responds to economic pressure regardless of its origin. Communities of color have every structural advantage in this game: numbers, cultural solidarity, generational loyalty, and historical grievance that does not fade. The only question is whether we use it deliberately, with strategy, and with permanence.

Cultural Shifts: Changing Public Attitudes Toward Ethical Consumerism

In addition to its impact on corporate behavior, economic activism also shifts public attitudes about ethical consumerism. As more consumers adopt a mindset of intentional spending and strategic boycotting, the idea of purchasing as an act of resistance becomes more mainstream. The rise of conscious consumerism—characterized by a growing recognition that the products we buy have social, environmental, and economic consequences—is reshaping the marketplace. Brands that demonstrate genuine commitment to corporate social responsibility are gaining market share, while those that fail to meet consumer expectations are falling behind.

Building Wealth: Fostering Generational Financial Security

One of the most profound long-term effects of economic activism is its ability to foster generational wealth for marginalized communities. By supporting minority-owned businesses and local entrepreneurs, consumers can help create self-sustaining ecosystems that generate wealth, job opportunities, and long-term financial security. The National Black Chamber of Commerce (NBCC) has long advocated for the economic empowerment of Black businesses, creating spaces for Black entrepreneurs to thrive and promoting the importance of buying Black.

Conclusion: The Ripple Effect of Economic Activism

The ripple effect of economic activism is far-reaching. By holding corporations accountable, shifting public attitudes toward ethical consumerism, and supporting minority-owned businesses, consumers are creating a new, more just economic landscape. Your dollars have power, and when you choose to spend them in ways that align with your values, you are helping to build a future where economic empowerment and social justice go hand in hand.

Chapter 8: When Boycotting Isn't Enough

$ $ $

Permanent boycotting has proven to be a powerful tool for social and economic change. But there are moments when it is not enough to rely solely on the act of withholding consumer support. In today's complex, globalized economy, there will always be corporations, industries, and systems that are difficult or even impossible to boycott entirely. In many cases, these entities hold a level of control over essential services or products that make full-scale boycotting an unrealistic option for many consumers.

So, what do we do when boycotting alone cannot deliver the transformation we seek? In this chapter, we explore how to build a broader, more effective strategy for economic activism that goes beyond the binary of "boycotting or buying." It is a call for a multi-pronged approach—one that emphasizes not only the strategic withdrawal of support from harmful corporations but also the creation of sustainable alternatives and advocacy for systemic changes.

The Challenges of Full-Scale Boycotting

We live in an interconnected world where supply chains are sprawling and monopolistic practices are common. Some of the companies we wish to avoid are so embedded in the fabric of our daily lives that cutting them out entirely is nearly impossible. Consider the sheer size and influence of tech giants like Apple, Google, Amazon, and Microsoft. For many consumers, choosing to boycott these companies means giving up essential services, from communication tools to entertainment to basic commerce.

In industries like food and agriculture, where a few large corporations control the majority of production and distribution, completely avoiding certain companies is no small feat. Take sprawling food conglomerates like Nestlé and Unilever, which not only produce food directly but own brands across multiple sectors. In these cases, boycotting specific brands can still result in unintentional support of their parent companies. Nestlé alone owns more than two thousand brands globally—from infant formula and bottled water to pet food and ice cream. Fully boycotting Nestlé would require ongoing research, planning, and sustained attention.

Despite the significant challenge that large-scale boycotts present, the complexity does not justify abandoning the effort. It requires us to consider not just which companies we boycott, but how we adapt our purchasing behavior overall—and how we build alternatives that reduce our dependence on these systems over time.

Economic Intention: More Than Just Avoiding Problematic Companies

It's vital to shift the conversation from a passive act of merely avoiding problematic corporations to a more active, intentional approach to spending. Economic intention is about making conscious, informed choices that reflect your values—not just avoiding what you don't support, but actively seeking out alternatives that align with your goals of equity and justice.

Instead of simply saying "no" to a company's harmful practices, economic intention involves saying "yes" to businesses that reflect the change you wish to see. Supporting companies like Patagonia, known for its environmental activism and commitment to fair labor practices, or Ben & Jerry's, which has consistently and publicly advocated for racial justice—you are actively investing in organizations that treat their values as operational commitments rather than marketing strategies.

Spending Strategically: Filling the Gaps with Alternatives

In cases where full-scale boycotting may not be feasible, strategic spending involves seeking out businesses that meet your needs while adhering to ethical standards. For technology, choosing companies like

Fairphone—committed to ethical sourcing of materials—can make a significant difference even if you cannot exit the tech ecosystem entirely. In retail, clothing, and food, many local or grassroots alternatives provide the same products as larger corporations without the ethical complications.

Building the Alternative Economy: What It Actually Looks Like

While individual acts of boycotting, intentional spending, and advocacy are critical, the long-term vision requires something larger: building an alternative economic structure rooted in values of equity, sustainability, and community empowerment.

Credit unions represent one of the most immediately accessible entry points. Unlike major banks, credit unions are member-owned, nonprofit financial institutions that return profits to members in the form of lower fees and better interest rates. They are not beholden to shareholders or driven by the profit motive that has led major banks to engage in predatory lending and discriminatory financial practices.

Community Land Trusts (CLTs) offer another model. A CLT is a nonprofit organization that acquires and holds land in permanent trust for the benefit of a community, ensuring that housing and commercial space remain affordable and community-controlled even as surrounding property values rise. CLTs have been particularly effective in preventing displacement in gentrifying neighborhoods—keeping land in the community instead of allowing it to be captured by speculative real estate interests.

Consumer and worker cooperatives—like Cooperation Jackson and the hundreds of food co-ops across the country—demonstrate that the cooperative model can function at scale across many industries. The cooperative structure places ownership, decision-making, and profit distribution in the hands of the people who work in and use the enterprise. There are over 30,000 cooperatives in the

United States, with over $650 billion in revenue annually. This is not a fringe idea. It is a growing economic sector that needs our participation and support.

These alternatives are not perfect or complete. They cannot yet replace the full range of goods and services provided by the corporate economy. But they are growing. And every purchase, every deposit, every membership that flows into these structures makes them stronger and more capable of providing genuine alternatives.

Navigating Complex Systems: Finding Practical Approaches

Join or create consumer cooperatives to pool resources and make collective purchasing decisions. Engage in corporate advocacy—contact companies directly, sign petitions, and demand accountability through their social media channels. We cannot pretend that every purchase we make will be perfect. But we can strive to minimize our dependence on systems that perpetuate injustice while building the alternatives that will eventually make that dependence unnecessary.

Conclusion: Beyond Boycotting—A New Economic Vision

Boycotting, while powerful, is not a cure-all. But when paired with intentional spending, advocacy, and the deliberate construction of alternative economic infrastructure, boycotting becomes part of a larger vision—a vision where we not only withdraw support from harmful corporations but actively build the economy we wish to see.

When boycotting isn't enough, we push forward with intention. We shift from simply opposing harmful practices to actively creating a new, more equitable economic system. We become architects of an economic landscape where our values—justice, equity, and sustainability—shape the marketplace. The fight for economic empowerment is a marathon, not a sprint. And every dollar spent with intention is a step toward building a better, fairer world for us all.

Chapter 9: Economic Activism Across Generations

$ $ $

The movement does not sustain itself. It is taught.

Economic resistance has been passed down through Black families for generations—not always in formal lessons, but in the stories told at dinner tables, in the quiet decisions of grandmothers who refused to shop where they were disrespected, in the aunts who drove past a closer store to give their money to the Black-owned one two neighborhoods over. These were not accidents. They were acts of transmission. Someone taught them. And they chose to teach the next generation.

We are at a moment when that transmission needs to become explicit. Our children are growing up inside an economy that is designed to make them consumers before they are conscious. The algorithm knows what they want before they ask. Brand loyalty is cultivated in childhood. By the time a young person is eighteen, they have been marketed to for more than a decade—and have rarely been asked to consider whether the companies marketing to them deserve their money. That changes when we make it a conversation.

Starting the Conversation at Home

You do not need an economics degree to teach a child about money and power. You need a grocery store and a question.

The next time you are shopping with your child or grandchild, ask them: "Do you know who owns this store?" Most children—and most adults—have never considered it. Follow with: "Do you know if they hire people who look like us in leadership positions? Do they support our community?" You don't need to have all the answers. The questions are the lesson.

For older children and teenagers, the conversation can go deeper. Talk about the companies on the DO NOT BUY list and explain why they're there—not as punishment or drama, but as information. Explain what DEI means in plain language: Does this company treat people fairly? And when given the chance to publicly commit to fairness, did they choose to? Let your teenager research a company before you make a purchase. Give them the job of finding an ethical alternative. Make them part of the decision. This is not just an exercise—it is a transfer of knowledge and agency.

These conversations do something else: they show children that adults take their values seriously enough to act on them. That modeling is more powerful than any formal lesson.

Teaching Economic Literacy as Liberation

Economic literacy—understanding how money moves, who benefits from where it goes, and how to use spending as a tool—is not taught in most schools. It is certainly not taught as a justice practice. We teach children what things cost. We do not often teach them what their spending costs the community, or what it could build if redirected.

Beyond conversations about specific companies, families and communities can teach young people the following principles:

Every dollar has a direction. Where it goes shapes what exists. The question is not just whether you can afford something, but what you are building by purchasing it.

Ownership matters. The difference between a customer and an owner is power. Learning to ask "who owns this?" before every major purchase is the beginning of a new relationship with the economy.

Collective action is possible. One person redirecting spending is a preference. One hundred people redirecting spending is a statement. One thousand people redirecting spending is a movement. And movements change things.

This is a tradition. Greenwood existed. The grape boycott happened. The people of Montgomery walked to work for 381 days. We come from people who understood economic power and used it. We are not inventing something new. We are continuing something old.

When young people understand that economic activism is not a new idea but an inherited one—that they are part of a long line of people who chose where to spend as an act of dignity—it stops being a sacrifice and starts being an identity.

Youth and Social Media as Boycott Infrastructure

The generation coming up now has tools their grandparents could not have imagined. A teenager with a smartphone can research a company's labor practices, share a boycott call with ten thousand followers, find an ethical alternative, and complete the purchase—all in twenty minutes. What once required union halls and printed pamphlets now happens in a group chat.

Young people have already demonstrated their willingness to use these tools for economic activism. The resurgence of #BuyBlack movements after each new corporate betrayal shows that younger consumers are not passive—they are building the infrastructure of the next generation of boycotts in real time. Platforms like TikTok have hosted powerful consumer education content, with creators explaining supply chains, exposing corporate greenwashing, and directing followers toward ethical alternatives.

But social media boycotts face a specific danger: they peak fast and fade faster. A company can weather a week of viral outrage. What companies cannot weather is the quiet, sustained withdrawal of consumers who simply never come back. The task for young economic activists is to convert the energy of digital mobilization into the discipline of permanent redirection. That bridge—from viral moment to lasting change—is built in community. Young people can launch a boycott in an afternoon. The adults in their lives help them hold it.

Raising Economic Activists: Practical Starting Points

With younger children (ages 6–10): Make shopping a learning experience. Talk about where food comes from. Practice reading labels. Ask "is this made locally?" and explain why that matters. Let children help choose between two products based on what you know about the companies.

With tweens (ages 11–13): Introduce the concept of corporate values. Look up a company's DEI record together before a birthday purchase. Discuss what it means that a company profits from your community. Help them identify one Black-owned business in each category they regularly spend in.

With teenagers (ages 14–18): Have the full conversation about the DO NOT BUY list and why. Encourage them to research companies for the family. Give them agency in household spending decisions that relate to the boycott. Talk about credit, banking, and why the family's money is in the financial institution it's in.

With young adults (18+): Talk about the specific power they're about to have—their first job, their first bank account, their first apartment lease. Help them see that the habit of intentional spending is most easily established before convenience and routine have calcified around the default choices.

The Elders: Passing the Torch

Economic activism across generations is not only about passing knowledge down. It is also about listening up.

The elders in our communities carry memory that no book can fully hold. They remember which stores refused to hire Black workers. They remember which banks denied loans to Black families in neighborhoods that are now considered desirable real estate. They remember the boycotts that worked and the ones that didn't, and why. Creating space for those conversations—at family dinners, in community centers, in churches and mosques and community organizations—is itself an act of economic activism. It is the preservation of the institutional knowledge that makes sustained movements possible.

A movement with no memory is a movement that must reinvent itself after every setback. A movement with memory knows it has survived setbacks before. The most powerful economic activist in your family might be the grandmother who has been quietly spending with intention for fifty years without ever calling it by that name.

Conclusion: The Movement We Are Handing Forward

Every generation inherits an economy it did not design and is asked to survive inside systems it did not choose. What we can give the next generation is the consciousness to see those systems clearly, the tools to navigate them strategically, and the community to sustain the effort over time.

The movement does not sustain itself. We sustain it. And we sustain it by passing it forward—in conversations, in choices, in the stories we tell about who we are and what we value and how we have always fought for our dignity with our dollars as surely as with our words. Teach the children. Tell the stories. Make the choices visible. The revolution is not just ours. It belongs to everyone who comes after us—and they are watching what we do right now.

Conclusion: A Call to Action

Embracing Permanent Boycotting and Strategic Spending for Lasting Change

As we stand at a pivotal moment in history, the choices we make today will shape the future. The actions we take—or fail to take—will determine whether we continue to allow corporations and institutions to perpetuate harm, or whether we rise up to build a more just, equitable, and sustainable world. Permanent boycotting and strategic spending offer us the tools to turn our economic power into a force for positive change—a force that compels corporations to rethink their practices and ensures that marginalized communities no longer bear the burden of exploitation and inequity.

The heart of this book has been to remind us of our immense power as consumers—a power that can be wielded to dismantle systems of oppression and demand accountability. The economy is not a faceless, monolithic structure. It is made up of individual decisions, individual choices, and individual voices. Your voice. Your dollars. Your actions. Each of us has the power to make a difference, to redirect the flow of money from companies that exploit and harm to those that uplift, celebrate, and support our communities.

Permanent boycotting is not simply an act of resistance; it is an act of liberation. It is about reclaiming our economic autonomy, breaking free from the stranglehold that corporations have had on our spending habits, and choosing to support businesses that align with our values of justice, equity, and sustainability. It is about recognizing that we are not powerless in the face of corporate greed and government-backed discrimination. We are stronger than we realize. And when we stand united in our resolve, when we hold firm to our collective power, we can force even the largest corporations to reckon with the consequences of their actions.

As we have seen throughout this book, the consequences of rolling back anti-discrimination and DEI policies are not trivial—they are personal. These decisions affect real people—mothers, fathers, sons, daughters—who are tired of being seen as afterthoughts, tired of being marginalized in the very spaces where they are told they belong.

But the beauty of boycotting lies in its power to change the narrative. It is an act of defiance, yes—but it is also an act of creation. It is about building new relationships, forging new paths, and fostering a future where businesses thrive not on the exploitation of communities, but on the empowerment of them. We can choose to spend our dollars where they are celebrated, not just tolerated.

The work is not easy. It requires consistency, discipline, and courage. But let me tell you: every decision you make, every dollar you choose to spend intentionally, every boycott you maintain—these are powerful acts that ripple out and create lasting change. When we act together, when we unify in our purpose, we create a wave of transformation that no corporation can ignore.

Our collective economic resistance is a tool for liberation. By staying disciplined in our economic choices, by building lasting networks of support, and by educating future generations on the power of economic activism, we can create a world where justice, equity, and inclusion are not just buzzwords, but the foundation of a new and thriving economy.

The revolution starts with us. It starts now. It starts with you.

Where We Go From Here

1. This week, identify three companies you will no longer support and find one ethical alternative for each. Write them down. Make it real.
2. Move your checking or savings account to a Black-owned bank or local credit union. OneUnited, Greenwood Bank, and Carver Federal Savings Bank are places to start. This is the single most immediate structural action most readers can take.
3. Before your next major purchase, spend ten minutes researching the company's DEI record and ownership. Use the tools in Appendix F. Make the research a habit before the habit becomes automatic.
4. Bring one other person into this work. Share this book, share the conversation, share the resource lists. Economic activism scales through community. You are not meant to do this alone.
5. On Buy Black Friday, spend at least 25% of your holiday budget with Black-owned businesses. Make it 50%

the year after. Then stop waiting for November.

The Economic Empowerment Pledge

$ $ $

I pledge to support economic justice through permanent boycotting of companies that fail to uphold equity, inclusion, and anti-discrimination. I commit to redirecting my spending to businesses that align with my values and uplift marginalized communities.

I understand that my financial choices have power. I will educate myself, my family, and my community, and remain consistent in this practice to help create a more just and equitable economy. I will not return to companies that have betrayed my community's trust without evidence of genuine, structural, and sustained change.

I will stay the course. I will hold the line. I will build something better with every dollar I redirect.

Signature: ______________________________

Date: __________________

One commitment I make today:

____

Appendix A: Boycott Resource Guide

This resource guide is designed to help individuals, families, and communities plan, launch, and sustain permanent boycotts with intention, discipline, and measurable impact.

Boycott Planning—Key Steps

1. Identify companies to boycott using news sources, DEI accountability reports, and tracking tools.
2. Research the specific reasons: document DEI rollbacks, discriminatory behavior, or broken commitments.
3. Identify alternative businesses—preferably local, minority-owned, or ethically committed brands.

4. Inform your network: share reasons, resources, and alternatives with family and community.
5. Set goals: track weekly and monthly spending redirection and review quarterly.

Family and Community Engagement Tips

- Host monthly Economic Empowerment Nights to share updates, new resources, and alternative businesses.
- Create social media pages or group chats dedicated to holding businesses accountable and sharing ethical alternatives.
- Build and maintain a "Buy Black and Ethical" business directory specific to your city or neighborhood.
- Partner with local Black-owned businesses to host community marketplace events.

Appendix B: Conscious Spending Guide

Intentional Spending Checklist

Before making a significant purchase, work through the following questions:

- Have I researched this company's DEI and equity practices?
- Is this business minority-owned, locally owned, or ethically certified?
- Does this purchase align with my stated values?
- Are there local or sustainable alternatives available?
- Can I delay the purchase and invest time in finding a better source?
- If this is a necessity and no ethical alternative exists, is there a way to

minimize the purchase or reduce dependence over time?

Weekly Spending Reflection—Questions to Ask Yourself

- Three purchases I made this week that I'm proud of—and why.
- One area where I defaulted to convenience over values—and what I'll try differently next time.
- One new ethical alternative I discovered this week.
- One person I shared this practice with.

Appendix C: Community Accountability Guide

Monthly Accountability Tracking —What to Measure

Tracking your progress over time reinforces the practice and reveals where you're strongest and where you need more support. Consider reviewing the following each month:

- Boycotts maintained this month—which companies did you successfully avoid?
- New conscious purchases made—which ethical businesses did you discover or support?

- Money redirected—how much did you redirect from boycotted brands to ethical alternatives?
- Community impact—did you share resources, bring someone into the practice, or support a community event?
- Lessons learned—what challenged you? What worked well?

Building Your Community Accountability Circle

Consider organizing a group of three to five friends, family members, or neighbors who commit to the same practice and check in monthly. Share your tracking, your wins, your challenges, and your discoveries. Accountability circles have been shown to dramatically improve sustained behavior change in almost every domain—and economic activism is no exception.

Appendix D: Black-Owned and Ethical Business Directory (Starter List)

This starter directory highlights Black-owned, Indigenous, People of Color (BIPOC)-owned, and ethical businesses you can support. It is by no means exhaustive and should be supplemented by local research and live-updated online directories. Check WeBuyBlack (webuyblack.com) and Official Black Wall Street (officialblackwallstreet.com) for regularly updated listings.

Online Marketplaces

- WeBuyBlack (webuyblack.com)—The largest online marketplace for Black-owned businesses.
- Official Black Wall Street (officialblackwallstreet.com)—A discovery tool for Black-owned businesses across the country.
- Miiriya (miiriya.com)—Marketplace supporting Black-owned vendors with no seller fees.

Financial Institutions

- OneUnited Bank—Nation's largest Black-owned bank.
- Greenwood Bank—Digital banking for Black and Latino communities.
- Carver Federal Savings Bank—Based in Harlem, NYC, with a focus on underserved communities.
- Your local credit union—Find one at mycreditunion.gov.

Beauty and Wellness

- The Lip Bar—Vegan and cruelty-free makeup brand.
- Briogeo—Haircare line focused on clean, effective formulas.
- Golde—Superfood-based wellness and skincare brand.

Food and Beverage

- Partake Foods—Allergy-friendly cookies and snacks.
- McBride Sisters Wine Company—One of the largest Black-owned wine companies in the world.
- Trade Street Jam Co.—Small-batch, flavor-forward preserves.

Home Goods

- Clare Paint—Zero-VOC paint in curated designer colors.
- Estelle Colored Glass—Luxury hand-blown colored glassware.
- Effie's Paper—Modern stationery and lifestyle brand centering Black women.

Media and Publishing

- Haymarket Books—Progressive, independent publishing house.
- Black Classic Press—Publishes works by and about people of African descent.
- MahoganyBooks—Bookstore dedicated to Black authors and readers.

Appendix E: Legislative Advocacy and Policy Toolkit

Individual consumer action is essential. But lasting structural change also requires engaging with the systems of law and policy that shape the corporate landscape. This toolkit is designed to help you engage with policymakers and advocate for legislative protection of DEI and anti-discrimination efforts.

Sample Advocacy Email

Subject: Support DEI and Anti-Discrimination Legislation

Dear [Elected Official's Name],

As a constituent of [City, State], I am writing to express my deep concern over the rollback of diversity, equity, and inclusion (DEI) initiatives by major corporations. The dismantling of these efforts sends a dangerous message that our communities and values are no longer welcome in the marketplace. I urge you to take immediate action to support legislation that ensures these protections remain in place.

[Insert personal story or specific call to action.]

Sincerely,

[Your Name]

Call Script for Elected Officials

Hello, my name is [Your Name], and I'm a constituent from [City, State]. I am calling today to urge you to support policies that protect DEI initiatives and prevent corporations from rolling back their commitments to racial equity and inclusion. The dismantling of these policies is harmful to marginalized communities and has long-term negative consequences for social and economic justice in our community. I would like to know your position on this issue. Thank you for your time.

Advocacy Organizations to Follow or Join

- Color of Change—colorofchange.org
- Public Citizen—citizen.org
- NAACP Legal Defense Fund—naacpldf.org
- Center for American Progress—americanprogress.org
- National Minority Supplier Development Council—nmsdc.org

Appendix F: Digital Boycott and Consumer Tracking Tools

Technology can be your ally in sustaining long-term boycotts and promoting intentional, values-aligned spending.

Apps and Tools for Ethical Spending

- Buycott—Scan product barcodes to uncover company affiliations and parent companies.
- DoneGood—Ethical shopping platform featuring sustainable and mission-driven brands.
- Good On You—Rates fashion brands based on labor, sustainability, and ethics.

- Progressive Shopper—Shows corporate political donations and affiliations.
- Yuka—Rates food and cosmetic products based on health and ingredient transparency.

Tips for Tracking and Sustaining Your Impact

1. Use budgeting apps and add spending tags like "Black-Owned," "Local," or "Boycotted" to track your progress.
2. Set monthly goals—commit a percentage of your monthly spending to Black-owned or ethical businesses and increase it over time.
3. Maintain a shared boycott list with your community—a cloud-shared document works well for communal tracking and updates.
4. Build reward loops—treat yourself with a monthly purchase from a Black-owned business as a milestone celebration.
5. Stay educated and connected—subscribe to newsletters or alerts from

watchdog outlets, advocacy groups, and ethical brands.

Appendix G: Starter "DO NOT BUY" List

The following is an alphabetical list of companies that have either rolled back or dismantled their anti-discrimination and/or Diversity, Equity, and Inclusion (DEI) policies. This list includes parent companies and selected subsidiaries. It is current as of the time of publication and should be supplemented with ongoing research, as corporate policies change.

A

1. 3M
2. Accenture
3. Adobe
4. Aldi
5. Airbnb

6. Amazon (Ring, Audible, Zappos, Whole Foods, IMDb, Goodreads)
7. Amtrak

B

8. Bank of America
9. BJ's Wholesale
10. BlackRock
11. Boeing
12. Booz Allen
13. Bristol Myers Squibb

C

14. Caterpillar
15. Chan Zuckerberg Initiative
16. Charter Communications
17. Citigroup

D

18. Deloitte

F

19. Ford

G

20. GameStop
21. GE Aerospace
22. GM
23. Goldman Sachs
24. Google

H

25. Harley-Davidson

I

26. IBM

J

27. Jack Daniel's
28. John Deere

L

29. Lockheed Martin
30. Lowe's

M

31. Macy's
32. Major League Baseball (MLB)
33. Marriott
34. McDonald's
35. Meta (Facebook, Instagram)
36. Molson Coors

N

37. Nestlé (Alpo, Fancy Feast, Beneful, Gerber, Coffeemate, Perrier, Hot Pockets, Lean Cuisine, Stouffer's, Häagen-Dazs, Nature's Bounty, and more)
38. Nissan
39. Nordstrom
40. Northrop Grumman

P

41. Paramount (CBS, BET, MTV, Nickelodeon, Showtime, VH1, Comedy Central, Smithsonian Channel)
42. PepsiCo
43. RTX (Raytheon Technologies)

S

44. Salesforce
45. Shopify
46. SpaceX
47. Stanley Black & Decker
48. Starbucks
49. State Street

T

50. T-Mobile
51. Target
52. Tesla
53. Toyota
54. Tractor Supply

U

55. UBS
56. Uber
57. Unilever (Dove, Hellmann's, Knorr, Magnum, POND'S, Paula's Choice, TRESemmé, and more)
58. UnitedHealth Group

V

59. Vanguard
60. Victoria's Secret

W

61. Walmart
62. Walt Disney Company
63. Washington Metropolitan Area Transit Authority (Metro)
64. Wells Fargo

Z

65. Zoom

Sources and Notes

The following sources inform the data, case studies, and historical references throughout this book. Readers are encouraged to engage with these resources directly and to continue their own research as corporate policies and economic conditions evolve.

Chapter 1: Economic Resistance as a Movement

- Greenberg, Cheryl. "Or Does It Explode?": Black Harlem in the Great Depression. Oxford University Press, 1991. (Harlem "Don't Buy Where You Can't Work" movement)
- King, Martin Luther Jr. Stride Toward Freedom: The Montgomery Story. Harper & Row, 1958.

- United Farm Workers. The History of the UFW. ufw.org.
- Gibbs, Sara. "Nike's Labor Practices: The Evolution of a Corporate Response." Business and Human Rights Journal, 2017.

Chapter 2: The Power of Minority Spending

- Selig Center for Economic Growth, University of Georgia. Multicultural Economy Report. Terry College of Business, 2023.
- Nielsen. Diverse Intelligence Series: African American Consumers. Nielsen Holdings, 2023.
- McKinsey & Company. "The Black Consumer: Unearthing Signals for Inclusive Growth." 2021.
- McKinsey & Company. "Diversity Wins: How Inclusion Matters." 2020.

Chapter 3: Corporate DEI Retreats in 2025

- Human Rights Campaign. Corporate Equality Index 2024–2025. hrc.org.
- Edelman Trust Barometer: Special Report on Business and Racial Justice. 2023.
- Murphy, Laura W. Facebook Civil Rights Audit: Final Report. July 2020.
- Various news sources documenting 2024–2025 corporate DEI rollbacks, including The New York Times, The Washington Post, NPR, and the Associated Press.

Chapter 4: The Permanence of Boycotting

- Multiple news reports tracking Goya Foods market performance, 2020–2024.
- Associated Press. "Papa John's Founder John Schnatter Resigns from Board of Directors." November 2018.

Chapter 5: Staying the Course

- Messer, Chris M., Thomas E. Shriver, and Alison E. Adams. "The Destruction of Black Wall Street: Tulsa's 1921 Riot and the Eradication of Accumulated Wealth." American Journal of Economics and Sociology, 2018.

- Anderson, Maggie. Our Black Year: One Family's Quest to Buy Black in America's Racially Divided Economy. PublicAffairs, 2012. (Buy Black Friday)

Chapter 6: Shopping with Intention

- Cooperation Jackson. cooperationjackson.org.
- National Credit Union Administration. mycreditunion.gov.

Chapter 7: The Ripple Effect of Economic Activism

- Color of Change. "Starbucks and Racial Bias: Our Demands and Why They Matter." 2018. colorofchange.org.
- Chesto, Jon. "Wayfair Employees Stage Walkout Over Sales to Migrant Detention Centers." Boston Globe, June 2019.

- Byron, Ellen. "Bud Light's Stumble and the New Rules of Brand Activism." The Wall Street Journal, 2023.

Chapter 8: When Boycotting Isn't Enough

- National Center for Employee Ownership. nceo.org.
- Community Land Trust Network. cltnetwork.org.
- US Federation of Worker Cooperatives. usworker.coop.

Chapter 9: Economic Activism Across Generations

- Anderson, Maggie. Our Black Year. PublicAffairs, 2012.
- Pew Research Center. "Teens and Social Media." 2023. pewresearch.org.

About the Author

M Tucker Cunningham is a passionate writer, cultural analyst, and literary activist who is deeply committed to using her platform to address social justice, economic empowerment, and the importance of representation in media. Born and raised in New York City, she has spent her career advocating for the voices of marginalized communities, particularly within the realms of education, culture, and media.

With a background in psychology and education, Cunningham uses her unique perspective to explore the intersections of race, media, and representation. As a mother and an intellectual, she is dedicated to amplifying the narratives of Black women throughout history, championing diverse and transformative media representation, and fostering an environment where social activism and economic change intersect.

Cunningham's work spans several genres, including books on economic empowerment, transformative media, poetry, and children's literature that teaches lessons about inclusivity, kindness, and environmental awareness.

Her advocacy extends beyond her writing, as she actively works with organizations that promote media literacy, anti-violence efforts, and the empowerment of Black creatives. Her dedication to the betterment of her community and society as a whole drives everything she does.

In her free time, Tucker enjoys gardening, spending time with her cats, and continuing to explore ways in which we can build a more equitable and inclusive world through both small and large actions.

www.ingramcontent.com/pod-product-compliance
Lightning Source LLC
LaVergne TN
LVHW010319220926
848484LV00004BB/791
* 9 7 8 1 9 7 2 5 3 9 1 4 9 *